STARTING · WITH · S

science fair

PLANTS

By · THE · ONTARIO · SCIENCE · CENTRE

PHOTOGRAPHS BY RAY BOUDREAU

KIDS CAN PRESS

J581
O58p

Published in Canada by
Kids Can Press Ltd.
29 Birch Avenue
Toronto, ON M4V 1E2

Published in U.S. by
Kids Can Press Ltd.
85 River Rock Drive, Suite 202
Buffalo, NY 14207

Written by Katharine Vanderlinden and Carol Gold
Edited by Valerie Wyatt
Designed by James Ireland/Peter Enneson

Printed in Hong Kong by Wing King Tong
Company Limited

CMC   94 0 9 8 7 6 5 4 3 2
CM PA 98 0 9 8 7 6 5 4 3 2

Canadian Cataloguing in Publication Data

Main entry under title:
Plants

(Starting with science)
Includes index.

ISBN 1-55074-193-4 (bound)   ISBN 1-55074-395-3 (pbk.)

1. Plants — Experiments — Juvenile literature.   2. Plants — Juvenile literature.   I. Boudreau, Ray.   II. Ontario Science Centre.   III. Series.

QK52.6.P53 1994   j581'.078   C94-931090-5

Kids Can Press is a Nelvana company

Table of contents

Seed sense

What would happen if you planted a seed upside down? Would the roots grow up in the air? Would the stem grow down into the ground? Find out by making a see-through garden.

You will need:

- 5 dried beans (any kind — from the supermarket or a seed packet)
- a piece of construction paper
  - a big glass jar with a wide mouth
  - paper towels

What to do:

1. Soak the beans in water overnight.
2. Line the inside of the jar with a piece of construction paper.
3. Stuff the middle of the jar with wet paper towels.
4. Push the beans between the construction paper and the glass of the jar. Space them out evenly. Put the beans in every which way — some lying on their side, some upright and some at an angle.
5. Put your see-through garden in a light place, but not in direct sunlight. Leave it for several days. Keep watering the paper towels to keep the construction paper moist.
6. After a few days, you will see roots growing out of one end of each bean and stems growing out of the other end. Are they growing in all different directions? Or are all the roots growing down, and all the stems growing up?
7. In about a week, the stems will sprout little green leaves. Now they are called seedlings. Lay the jar on its side. Watch the seedlings for a few more days. Do the stems bend up again and the roots down?

What's happening?

Plant roots grow down because they have chemicals in them that respond to the earth's gravity — an invisible force that pulls things toward the earth. Stems have other chemicals in them that make them grow up, away from the earth and toward the light. So it doesn't matter how you plant a seed — it will always send its roots down and its stem up.

Superseed!

Have you ever seen a dandelion or other weed growing up through a crack in the sidewalk? What's going on? See for yourself.

You will need:
- 8 –10 dried beans (any kind — from the supermarket or a seed packet)
- paper towels
- a shallow saucer
- a piece of paper

What to do:
1. Soak the beans in water overnight.
2. Pile four small pieces of paper towel on the saucer. Soak the paper towels with water.
3. Put the beans on top of the towels. Leave space between them.
4. Tear or cut a piece of paper big enough to cover most but not all of the saucer. Put the paper over the beans, but don't let it touch the wet paper towels or it will get soggy and saggy.
5. Put the saucer in a light place, but not in direct sunlight. Watch for a few days. Keep the paper towels moist.

Are the sprouting beans strong enough to lift the paper?

6. Try the experiment again using more beans. This time, put heavier paper over some of the beans and cardboard over the others. Does it still work?

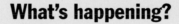

What's happening?

Plants grow upward, even if something is on top of them. And the growing tip is strong because it is filled with water. This water makes the plant strong enough to lift paper — and even break through a tiny crack in a cement sidewalk! Are you surprised that water can make plants so strong? Try filling a rubber glove with water. See how much stronger the fingers are when they are full of water?

Recycle a potato

Have you ever wondered why potatoes have eyes — those little round dents all over the potato? Next time you have potatoes, cut out some potato eyes and recycle them into a new potato plant.

You will need:

- a flower pot filled with potting or garden soil
- some raw potato eyes with a bit of extra potato around them

What to do:

1. Pat the soil down in the pot and water it well.

2. Press the potato eyes into the soil. Space them about 4 cm (1½ inches) apart. Cover them lightly with soil.

3. Put the pot in a light place, but not in direct sunlight. Keep the soil moist but not wet. In a few days your potato eyes will sprout leaves, and you will have some baby potato plants.

What's happening?

Each potato eye is a seed. When you plant it, it sprouts into a new potato plant. If you move your small potato plants into a big pot or garden, they should produce potatoes.

Make your scrap garden grow

Try planting a carrot top or some seeds from a green pepper. You can grow a whole garden of greenery. To recycle an avocado, use toothpicks to keep the bottom of the pit just touching the water, as shown above.

A dirt-free garden

How do you grow a garden without dirt? Hydroponically. What's that? Make your own hydroponic garden and see.

You will need:

- a sharp pencil
- a Styrofoam cup
- a glass jar with a wide mouth (the Styrofoam cup should just fit in the mouth of the jar as shown)
  - an old cotton rag about 20 x 20 cm (8 x 8 inches)
  - vermiculite (from a garden store)
  - hydroponic fertilizer (from a garden store)
  - seeds (radishes, lettuce, peas work best)

What to do:

1. Use the pencil to poke a large hole in the bottom of the Styrofoam cup.
2. Roll the rag up tightly.
3. Push one end of the rolled-up rag through the hole in the Styrofoam cup until it is about two-thirds of the way into the cup.

4. Fill the cup with vermiculite around the rolled-up rag.
5. Ask an adult to mix the hydroponic fertilizer with water. The package will tell you how much water.
6. Put some of this fertilizer liquid into the glass jar. Set the cup in the mouth of the jar with the rag hanging down into the liquid as shown in the big picture. The liquid should not touch the Styrofoam cup. If it does, pour some out.
7. Plant three seeds. The seed packet will tell you how deep.
8. Put your hydroponic garden in a sunny window. Make sure there's always enough liquid in the jar to keep the rag wet. In two or three weeks your seeds should sprout.

What's happening?

Plants need several things to grow and be healthy. First, they need to be anchored, so they won't blow or wash away. Usually the soil does this. In your hydroponic garden, vermiculite is the anchor. Plants also need food and water. Your fertilizer mixture provides both. When you add sunlight, your plants have everything they need.

A wet mystery

Have you ever wondered how water gets from a tree's roots all the way up to its leafy top? Try this to solve the mystery.

You will need:

- a small spoon
- blue food coloring
- a cup with 2.5 cm (1 inch) of water in it
- a butter knife
- a leafy stalk of celery

What to do:

1. Stir a spoonful of food coloring into the water in the cup.
2. Cut off the end of the celery stalk. Stand the stalk in the colored water.
3. Wait for an hour or two. What happens to the celery leaves?
4. Cut a stalk of celery lengthwise. The cut should stop just below the leaves. Put one half of the celery in blue-colored water and the other in red. Will the celery turn two colors?

What's happening?

The colored water traveled up tiny tubes inside the celery. Want to see the tubes? Take the celery out of the water and cut through the stalk. Do you see a row of tiny circles outlined in color? You have cut through long thin tubes that run up the stalk.

Trees have tubes, too, that go from the roots up the trunk and into the leaves. Water climbs up these tubes.

Why do plants need water?

From the time they are seeds, plants need water to grow. Water helps soften the outer covering of the seed so that the growing parts can break through. Then, as the plant grows, water travels up the tiny tubes from the roots to the leaves, where it is used to make food. Water also carries this food to all parts of the plant through another set of tubes. And water keeps the stem and leaves stiff. Without water, the plant would wilt.

A sour shower

Ever wonder what makes pickles taste sour? It's the vinegar they are soaked in. Vinegar is an acid. That acid doesn't do you any harm, but what about plants? Would they like acid? Try this and see.

You will need:

- 2 small potted plants (the same kind)
- a big spoon
- vinegar
- a measuring cup

What to do:

1. Put both plants in a bright spot for two weeks.

2. During this time, water one plant with tap water.

3. Water the other plant with vinegar water. To make it, mix a spoonful of vinegar into 250 mL (1 cup) of water. Label the container "vinegar water." If you run out, mix up some more.

4. Watch your plants. What happens to the plant that gets the vinegar water?

What's happening?

Plants need water to grow, but it must be clean water. Acid water kills them. If you kept on giving your plant vinegar, it would die. Try to save it by switching to pure water.

Acid rain and snow

Acid made your plant wilt. The same thing can happen to trees and plants outside. In many parts of the world, the rain contains an acid. The acid is made when gases from car engines and factories rise into the air and mix with rain and snow. When acid rain and acid snow fall back down to earth, they can kill trees, plants and pond life.

15

Stem bender

Plants need more than just water to grow. In fact, they can get all bent out of shape looking for something else they need. What is it? Try this and you'll see the light.

You will need:

- scissors
- a large cardboard box with a lid
- a small potted plant that fits inside the box

What to do:

1. Ask an adult to help you cut a hole about 8 cm (3 inches) wide in one side of the box.

2. Put the plant inside the box. Close the lid.

3. Put the box in a sunny spot. Water your plant just often enough to keep the soil moist.

4. After a week, look at your plant. What is happening to the stem?

5. Turn the box so that the hole faces another direction. Keep the plant facing the same way as before. Continue watering your plant.

6. After a week, look at the plant again.

What's happening?

Plants need sunlight and will try to reach it no matter what. When you put your plant in the box, the stem bends toward the light coming in through the hole. When you turn the box, the stem twists around to follow the sun again. If you kept turning the box, what would happen to the stem?

Why do plants need sunlight?

Light from the sun is one of the things green plants need to make their own food. The food is made by the leaves, using mainly sunlight, air and water. This amazing process is called photosynthesis. It is helped along by a chemical in the plant called chlorophyll, which also makes leaves green.

Milk carton composter

Just like you, plants need nutritious food to grow and be healthy. What do plants eat? Try feeding them your leftovers.

You will need:
- a clean empty cardboard milk carton
- waterproof tape
- scissors
- vegetable peels or other fruit and vegetable scraps
- a knife
- garden soil

What to do:
1. Seal the open end of the milk carton with tape.
2. Lay the milk carton on its side.
3. Ask an adult to cut a flap in the upper side big enough so you can reach inside with a spoon.
4. Save some peels and scraps left over from a meal. Use only fruit and vegetable scraps — no meat or dairy leftovers. Ask an adult to help you cut up the scraps into small pieces no bigger than your thumbnail.
5. Spread a thin layer of scraps over the bottom of the carton. Cover it with a thin layer of soil.
6. Each day, stir the mixture well and then add another layer of scraps and soil. Keep doing this every day until you've filled the carton to about 3 cm (1 inch) from the top.
7. Set the carton aside. Stir your mix every day for about three weeks. If it starts to get dry, add a bit of water but nothing else. Soon you'll have rich brown soil that is full of nutrients. Sprinkle it on plants in your house or garden as a special treat.

What's happening?
Invisible bacteria and fungi in the air and soil break down (rot) the vegetable scraps, and the nutrients (food) the scraps contained are absorbed by the plants.

A backyard composter works the same way as your milk carton composter. Leftovers, grass and other plant material rot and turn into nutritious soil.

Soil makers

Garden soil is full of tiny bacteria, as well as worms, bugs and other soil animals. These creatures help make healthy soil. How? They break down dead things by eating and digesting them. This puts nutrients (food) back into the soil. And they dig tunnels that allow in water and air, which plants also need to grow.

Make some dirt

In nature, it takes hundreds of years to make soil. How long would it take you? Try it and see.

You will need:

- a pail
- a cup full of sand
- a cup full of peat moss (from a hardware or garden store)
- a cup full of plant leftovers (such as cut-up fruit or vegetable skins, tea leaves, coffee grounds)
- a few broken eggshells
- water
- a large spoon

What to do:

1. Put the sand in the pail.

2. Add the peat moss. It will make the soil richer and help hold water.

3. Add the plant leftovers and broken eggshells, which provide nutrients plants need.

4. Add some water and mix it all together with the spoon. *Presto!* You've got soil.

Is it really soil?

To find out, see if a plant will grow in it. Put some of your soil in a pot and plant some radish seeds in it. Put the pot in a light place and keep it moist. Do the radishes sprout and grow? Soil is a mixture of minerals such as sand (which is really ground-up rocks), rotting plant and animal material, water and air. Your soil has all those things.

Why do plants need soil?

Soil provides support for plants, so they don't get washed or blown away. It also holds food and water for plants until they need it.

Backward garden

If you left a pair of socks outdoors one summer, what do you think you'd find the next spring? Try planting a sock and see. Plant a sock? Yes — and while you're at it, why not plant some other strange stuff, too?

Plant some or all of these things:

- an old nylon stocking or piece of pantyhose
- some cotton cloth (an old sock or piece of towel will do, but make sure it is 100% cotton)
- a piece of newspaper
- some plastic wrap
- some wool
- a Styrofoam or plastic cup
- a piece of aluminum foil
- an apple core

What to do:

1. Dig a hole 12 cm (5 inches) deep for each thing you are planting.

2. Pour enough water into each hole to make the soil damp but not muddy. Place one item in each hole. Cover it with dirt. Put a marker at each hole so you can find it later. Use small sticks or stones for markers.

3. Water your backward garden every day for one month. At the end of that time, dig it up. Has anything changed?

What's happening?

Some of the items you "planted" have started to fall apart and rot. Other items look just the same. That's because bacteria and other creatures in the soil break some things down over time, but not others. Things that *do* break down are said to be biodegradable. Which of the things on the table do you think are biodegradable?

Is it a plant?

Have you ever seen a mushroom growing? It looks like a plant, but it isn't. It's a fungus. Here's how to grow a type of fungus called mold.

You will need:

- a paper towel
- a clean pie plate
- a piece of bread
- plastic wrap
- a magnifying glass (if you have one)

What to do:

1. Wet the paper towel and lay it on the pie plate.

2. Put the bread on top.

3. Cover the plate with plastic wrap. Leave it in a dark place for a few days.

4. Look at the bread through the plastic wrap. Use a magnifying glass if you have one. What do you see? When you're done, don't eat the bread — **throw it away!**

What's happening?

The blue and white fuzzy stuff is mold. It grew from tiny spores that floated in the air and landed on the bread. Molds and other fungi can't make their own food like plants can. They have to feed on something else — such as your bread!

Seed stroll

Have you ever seen burrs or dandelion puffs sticking to a dog or cat's fur? Those plant hitchhikers are seeds. You can collect seeds just by taking a stroll. The best time is late summer or early fall.

You will need:
- a large pair of old wool socks
- tweezers
- a magnifying glass (if you have one)

What to do:
1. Put the socks on over your shoes.
2. Go for a walk around your yard. Or ask a parent to take a walk with you in a park or woods. Carefully brush your socks against some plants so that some seeds stick to them.
3. When you get home, use the tweezers to pick off the seeds sticking to your socks. Take a close look at the seeds. Use a magnifying glass if you have one. How many different kinds of seeds did you get? Do you know which plants or trees they came from?

What is a seed?
A seed is the part of a plant that grows into a new plant. Inside each seed is an embryo with a very tiny root and stem. All the seed needs to grow into a plant is some soil, sun and water.

The embryo is inside the seed.

Seeds come in all sizes. Some are so small you can hardly see them. The biggest ones — the seeds of the double coconut tree — can weigh as much as you do! But the size of a seed is no clue to how big the plant will be. The tallest plant in the world — the giant redwood tree — starts out with a seed smaller than your thumbnail.

Leaf hunt

Leaves come in all sorts of shapes and sizes. Why not make a leaf scrapbook to show off their shapes?

You will need:

- old newspapers
- some books
- transparent tape
- a scrapbook

What to do:

1. Go on a leaf hunt. Collect as many different kinds of leaves as you can. (Ask before you take leaves from garden or house plants.)

2. Sort the leaves into piles of similar shapes. See the picture for some common shapes.

3. Press the leaves you want to keep between pieces of newspaper. Pile some books on top and wait a week, until the leaves are flat and dry.

4. Tape the leaves into the scrapbook. Group leaves of similar shapes together.

5. Use a plant book to try to find out the names of some of the plants your leaves came from.

What do leaves do?

Leaves have a big job — they are food factories. Leaves make most of the food that plants need to live and grow. They make it using carbon dioxide (a gas) from the air, light from the sun, and water and nutrients (food) from the soil. The leaves contain chlorophyll, which makes them green.

For parents and teachers

Plants and seeds are a "user-friendly" way to introduce young children to basic biology. Here are some ideas to extend the activities in the book. The questions invite children to formulate a hypothesis and encourage open-ended experimentation.

Seed sense
What would happen if you turned the jar of sprouted seeds over every few days? Watch what happens to the roots and stems — do they still know which way is up? Plants' response to gravity is called geotropism and is controlled by plant hormones called auxins in the tip of the stem and root.

Superseed!
Will the beans continue to be strong as they grow? Plant the sprouting beans, three to a pot, and cover them with their paper weights. Plants aren't actually strong enough to break through solid concrete. They find a microscopic crack and push their way up through it.

Recycle a potato
Can other plants be recycled? Cut a leaf and a bit of stalk from an African violet and plant it in potting soil. Kept moist, it will send out roots. Take leaf and root cuttings from other house plants and see if they'll grow.

A dirt-free garden
Can you grow a hydroponic salad? Set up several hydroponic gardens and grow different vegetables in each. Try radish, lettuce, spinach, peas and green beans. Hydroponic comes from *hydro* meaning water and *geoponic*, having to do with agriculture. It is a useful growing method where the soil is poor.

A wet mystery
Would the celery turn a deeper color if you put more food coloring in the water? Put three similar-sized pieces of celery into three glasses, each with the same amount of water. Double the amount of food coloring in each glass. The process by which the colored water flows "up hill" in celery (and in trees) is called capillary action.

A sour shower
How acid is acid rain? Normal rain measures about 5 on the pH scale. In some parts of North America rain has been measured at 4.5 or lower — less acid than the vinegar water but still harmful to plants. Opposite to acids on the pH scale are substances called bases. Ammonia is very basic, about 11.1 on the pH scale. Water a healthy plant with a mixture of ammonia and water. (Caution: do not let children inhale ammonia fumes. Follow warnings on the ammonia bottle.) Does it do better than the plant watered with vinegar water?

Stem bender
Can plants grow in the dark? Put one plant in a sunny window and a similar-sized plant of the same species in a dark closet. Monitor their growth. Plants need light for photosynthesis, the process that converts water and carbon dioxide into food for the plant.

Milk carton composter, Make some dirt and Backward garden
Do all biodegradable things decompose at the same rate? Bury an orange peel and an apple peel in separate, marked holes. Dig up the two peels from time to time to see which rots first. Without lots of well-rotted organic matter, soil is just dirt.

Is it a plant?
Does mold like warmth? cold? sunshine? darkness? Place damp bread in a variety of places and see where mold grows best. Molds are neither plants nor animals. They are in a separate class of living things — fungi.

Seed stroll
How many kinds of seeds can you find around the house? All of these are seeds: dried beans, peas, corn, peanuts, soybeans, pumpkin seeds, poppy seeds, peppercorns, mustard seeds, coffee beans, sesame seeds, plus the seeds in fruits and vegetables.

Leaf hunt
How many different leaf shapes can you find? Don't forget odd shapes, such as evergreen needles and thick succulents. Try collecting flowers (most can be pressed, too), seeds and even roots. These parts serve the same functions in all plants — leaves produce food, flowers produce seeds, roots anchor the plant and collect water.

Words to know

acid: a substance that has a sharp, sour taste, like vinegar or lemon juice. A very strong acid can make your skin tingle or burn.

bacteria: tiny creatures in the soil or air that can break down (rot) animal or vegetable material

chlorophyll: the chemical in plants that makes leaves green. It is needed for photosynthesis.

embryo: a miniature form of a plant that is found in seeds. All plants begin their lives as an embryo.

fungi (plural): a group of living things that is neither plant nor animal. Mold
fungus (singular) and mushrooms are two kinds of fungi.

hydroponic garden: a garden that is grown in water rather than in soil

mold: a kind of fungus that grows on food, rotting plants and animals

nutrients: substances in food that plants and animals need to grow and be healthy

photosynthesis: the process by which green plants make their own food, using carbon dioxide (a gas in the air), light and water

seeds: a tiny baby plant, protected by a covering

spores: a kind of seed produced by a fungus

Index

acid, 14, 15
acid rain and snow, 15
avocados, 9

bacteria, 19, 23
beans, 4, 6, 7
biodegradable, 23

carbon dioxide, 29
celery, 12
chlorophyll, 16, 29
composters, 18

dirt. *See* soil

embryos, 26

fertilizer, 10, 11
food for plants, 11, 12, 18
food-making, 12, 16, 29
food scraps, 9, 18, 20
fungi, 18, 24

gardens
    backward, 22, 23
    hydroponic, 10, 11
    scrap, 9
    see-through, 4
gravity, 4

hydroponic gardens, 10, 11

leaf shapes, 28
leaves, 12, 16, 28, 29

magnifying glass, 24, 26
minerals, 21
molds, 24
mushrooms, 24

nutrients, 18, 19, 20, 29

peat moss, 20
photosynthesis, 16
potatoes, 8, 9

recycling, 8, 9
roots, 4, 12, 26
rotting, 18, 23

sand, 20, 21
seedlings, 4
seeds, 9, 10, 12, 21, 26
soil, 10, 11, 18, 20, 21, 23,
    26, 29
soil creatures, 19, 23
spores, 25
sprouting, 4, 9, 21
stems, 4, 12, 16, 26
sunlight, 4, 6, 8, 11, 16, 26,
    29

trees, 12, 15
trunks, 12
tubes, 12

vermiculite, 10, 11
vinegar, 14, 15

water, 7, 10, 11, 12, 14, 15,
    16, 26, 29
weeds, 6
wilting, 12, 15